THE PARADOX OF LOVE

A Jungian Look at The Dynamics of Life's Greatest Mystery

bright sky press
HOUSTON, TEXAS

2365 Rice Boulevard, Suite 202,
Houston, Texas 77005

10 9 8 7 6 5 4 3 2 1

ISBN 978-1-936474-09-7
Library of Congress Cataloging-in-Publication Data on file with publisher.
Printed in Canada.

Creative Direction, Ellen Peeples Cregan; Design, Marla Garcia;
Editorial Direction, Lucy Herring Chambers
Cover art by Merrilee McCommas McGehee

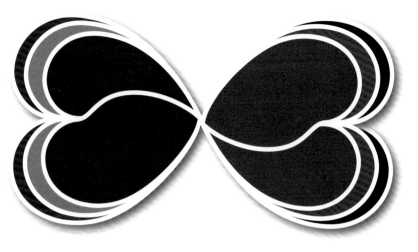

THE PARADOX OF LOVE

A Jungian Look at The Dynamics of Life's Greatest Mystery

J. Pittman McGehee, D.D.

To all those I have loved
and all those who have loved me

The most important
foundation of medicine is love.

– PARACELCUS

If it's not paradoxical, it's not true.

– SHUNRYU SUZUKI

TABLE OF CONTENTS

ACKNOWLEDGEMENTS **8**

INTRODUCTION **9**

CHAPTER 1
The Paradox of Love.................................. **15**

CHAPTER 2
Eros: A Creative Energy **21**

CHAPTER 3
Philia: Love of Kinship.............................. **31**

CHAPTER 4
Agape: Let It Be **39**

CHAPTER 5
The Archetypes of Love **45**

CHAPTER 6
Mother Love... **55**

CHAPTER 7
Too Much Or Not Enough?......................... **61**

CHAPTER 8
Father Love.. **69**

CHAPTER 9
The Father-Daughter Dynamic..................... **75**

CHAPTER 10
Discerning the Mystery **85**

CHAPTER 11
Ego Versus Self... **93**

CHAPTER 12
Self-Compassion....................................... **101**

CONCLUSION.. **107**

ACKNOWLEDGEMENTS

This reflective piece on love began as a series of lectures I presented at the C. G. Jung Educational Center in Houston. I would like to thank the staff of the Jung Center and acknowledge the Center for our long-time relationship. Further, I would like to thank all my students through the years who have helped me serve my purpose.

I truly wish to acknowledge my publisher, Bright Sky Press, most especially Lucy Chambers, Editorial Director, Tina Johnson, who transcribed hours of lectures and Cristina Adams for her clear and clean editing. The cover design was done by my very creative daughter-in-law, Merrilee McCommas McGehee. And I also want to thank Ellen Cregan, Creative Director, and Marla Garcia for implementing the cover art.

And as always, thank you to my family, who have been the primary empirical evidence that "those who dwell in love dwell in God and God in them." (I JOHN 4:16)

INTRODUCTION

WHEN I WAS A new seminarian, I initially read the first letter of John, wherein he writes: "God is love, and those who dwell in love, dwell in God, and God in them." Then, as a young priest, I first read C. G. Jung's autobiography, *Memories, Dreams, Reflections*. In a section called "Late Thoughts," Jung wrote some of the most beautiful prose I had ever read on the subject of love, wherein he names love as one of the "Greatest Mysteries." That statement of his is the backbone of this little book and the body of work that it represents.

With great insight into the obvious, I became aware that love is essential to the experience of being human; but if essential, what is its essence? This reflective work is the summation of a lifetime of thought, as a man,

11

son, brother, husband, father, and grandfather, vis-a-vis the greatest mystery.

If I falter at the task, it is a noble effort that will not fail if this reflection raises questions and expands consciousness. It would be grandiose to presume that this book could be definitive. But I believe it will be indicative of the depth and breadth of this inconceivable concept.

The first section engages the reality that the English language has only one word for love. Borrowing from Greek, we see that the words, Eros, Philia and Agape help in the expansion of our consciousness about different aspects of love. If nothing else, we discuss that love exists in the unity of a plurality of feelings. There are many aspects of love and yet paradoxically, there is a unity in the diversity of the several aspects.

The paradox of individuation—or of becoming whole—is *I alone must become myself, I cannot become myself alone.* Thus, the different experiences of the archetypal types of love help form and develop us in our process of becoming who we are.

We are shaped by those who love us and by those who refuse to love us. Or more importantly, we are formed by the psychopathologies that pretend to be love, that create low self-esteem, co-dependent behavior, lack of trust, defenses, fear and anxiety. So much of what we call love isn't; but rather, is neurotic projections, exploitations, manipulations and abuses.

To explore the four archetypal kinds of love: mother, father, other and Self, is to venture into the definitive loves one experiences in a natural life. Mother can nurture or consume, give life or smother; and, many times, she does both. Our discussion of mother love grants forgiveness to our biological mothers who could never fulfill our archetypal need for them.

Father love can empower or overpower. This energy called love, by the father principle, is that which can create a sense of competence and confidence or destroy one's sense of self-esteem and the ability to be an appropriately powerful presence of personality. Once again, we can forgive our fathers, as we only have humans to be our parents—not gods.

There ain't no magic other! And yet, we seek a significant other as a necessary love, in order to create and/or procreate. The other provides companionship in this difficult journey, and provides a mirror by which we might know ourselves more fully. The other is essential, but must not be expected to generate life or complete us. We must do that for ourselves.

The love of Self is not taught much or modeled in our culture. Self–love has been treated as auto-erotic or narcissistic and selfish. True self-love is an empowering self-compassion that can be as transforming as any externally generated love.

Eros, Philia, Agape: mother, father, other and Self are the three aspects and four kinds of love that provide a framework to discuss the paradox of love, one of life's greatest mysteries. I invite you to see this book not so much as a study, but as an experience of that which can only be known at a deeper level of knowing, where "God is love and those who dwell in love dwell in God, and God in them."

Chapter 1

THE PARADOX
OF LOVE

RYING TO TALK ABOUT AND understand the psychology of love is like trying to explore the Carlsbad Caverns with nothing but a penlight; you can make out some shapes, but little else. Indeed, discussing love is one of life's great paradoxes; it's something we can't do, but must do. Therein lies the paradox: the impossible challenge of coming up with words about Eros.

What is Eros? To me, it's that non-rational desire to connect, relate or create; Eros is, by its very definition, non-rational, and getting rational about love is one of the problems we have traditionally had in the Western world. As my mentor Robert Johnson, an author and noted Jungian analyst, likes to point out, you can tell the sophistication of a culture by the number of words it has for a concept. Eskimos, for example, have about fifty words for snow. In Sanskrit, there are seventy-eight words for love, but in our culture, we have only one, which shows how unsophisticated we are about the very sophisticated concept of love. We have the same word for how we feel about pizza as how we feel about spouses. For some that may be enough! I suspect that's because Western culture has been such a *logos* dominated culture, and that all the scientific, rational and industrial revolutions in our history have been dominated by the patriarchy.

Our whole idea of love has not been terribly sophisticated. It's not something we have studied very much because love is not particularly efficient, and efficiency is the God of capitalism. Love has its own economy and takes a long time to develop; it's very complicated, confusing and paradoxical. Moreover, few of us feel very confident talking about it. I have long been enamored by a quotation from French philosopher Pierre Teilhard de Chardin, who writes that, "Someday after mastering the winds, the waves, the tide, and gravity, we shall harness for God the energies of love, and then, for a second time in the history of the world, we will have discovered fire."

Still others speak of the conflict between the power of love versus the love of power. Interestingly, Jung felt that power, not hate or apathy, was the opposite of love. I've taught for years, and I have always thought that hate couldn't be the opposite of love because you can't hate somebody you don't love. Apathy, on the other hand, stands up better as an opposite. Sometimes you can't understand something until you understand its opposite. I struggled for years to understand grace, and what finally helped me understand it was disgrace. I don't think you can understand grace unless you have been disgraced, or had the experience of disgrace, or sat with somebody in the loneliness of disgrace. But it's not as if there is only one answer, one description or one conclusion to any of the speculations about this inequitable thing called love.

Trying to struggle with what is the opposite of love may help us frame some gestalt in the dark cavern that we have attempted to enter where fools fear to tread. We're looking and seeing a shape by looking at the opposite of love, and seeing that the opposite of love may be apathy. For once the libido shifts and leaves, it leaves a great vacuum. Jung believed that power fills the vacuum, power as in the desire to control, manipulate or dominate the need or desire to make somebody into something they weren't intended to be.

Let's start with a speculation by Jung that will be a sort of backdrop against which we walk around in the enormous cavern that is the concept of love. In his autobiography, *Memories, Dreams, Reflections*, Jung writes about love: "At this point, the fact forces itself on my attention that beside the field of reflection there is another equally broad, if not broader, area in which rational understanding and rational modes of representation find scarcely anything they are able to grasp. Reason cannot grasp; this is the realm of Eros. In classical times, when such things were properly understood, Eros was considered a god whose divinity transcended our human limits and who therefore could neither be comprehended nor represented in any way."

There's our task. It cannot be "comprehended nor represented in any way," but angels rush in where fools fear to tread. Jung goes on to note that, "I might, as many before me have attempted to do, venture an appropriate approach to this diamon, whose range of activity extends from the endless spaces of the heavens to the dark abyss of hell. But I falter before the task of finding the language, which might adequately express the incalculable paradoxes of love. Eros is a creator and father/mother of all higher consciousness." He's positing here the novel idea that love maybe an energy for creating consciousness. In other words, that Hallmark-card, cardboard Cupid version of love is inadequate. Love has more, perhaps greater, functions than simply the romanticized, idealized feeling we have come to understand as love. This is the backdrop against which we can begin to explore this cavern called "love." But remember that we have only a penlight, so we must be careful.

Chapter 2
EROS: A CREATIVE ENERGY

ACCORDING TO JUNG, our rational mind cannot possibly comprehend the breadth, depth and height of the paradox of love; for eons, poets and philosophers, psychologists and priests have tried to find ways to symbolize it and refer to it. Indeed, trying to talk about love has its own set of challenges, as there are many different shades of it: the love that a student has for a teacher or a teacher for a student, the love between people who haven't yet met or the patina-encrusted love of an older couple, to name a few. In the Greek tradition, there are four principal words for the concept of love: Eros (passionate love), Philia (friendship), Agape (true or unconditional love) and *Storge* (affection or familial love).

Let's begin with Eros, one of the most familiar

concepts of love. What is it really? I define Eros as a non-rational desire to connect, to relate or to create; it is both a common human experience and a part of <u>the</u> human experience. I believe it's also important to re-claim the word "love"—remember that Jung tried to use Eros to reclaim the word "Eros"—because it has been so misused and abused in popular culture, particularly in Hollywood where it has been identified with the erotic and sexualized love. Originally, Eros was thought to be a creation, a creative energy. Eros is spark, and Eros is a god. In the wonderful paradoxical way of myths, Eros is feminine and the god is masculine. However, in the myth of Psyche and Eros, Psyche is feminine and Eros is masculine.

I'm fond of saying that the creator has put a spark of the same creative energy that began the universe in every creature. So if we play with the idea that Eros was a creation, I suspect we can also think of that creative spark as numinous energy. Taken from a book titled *The Idea of the Holy*, the word "numinous" is reclaimed by the author Rudolf Otto as a synonym for God, en-ergy or power. The "numen" is creative energy, the kind that brings something into being that has never exist-ed before, or transforms in order to then generate and transform.

Within every human being, there is a creative urge or the urge to create. What happens in a relationship, if it's a healthy one, is the creation of something that has never been before. When two people are able to meet at this level of creativity, love or Eros, then that spark creates a whole that is greater than the sum of its two parts. Something is being added to creation or to a community of positive energy. The creation and community are expanded.

The urge to create something new isn't limited to relationships between human beings. We have Eros for an idea, we have Eros for communicating and creating through painting or writing or music. Sometimes we are even conduits for the Eros of God. In the first letter of John (1 JOHN 4:16), he says very profoundly that "God is love and he that dwells in love dwells in God, and God in him." As someone who comes from the Christian tradition that God is love, I think we're using God and love to describe the creative energy that creates or transforms a relationship, idea or symbol.

That creative energy can occur in a relationship, or it can come from within as a mighty diamon, as Jung called it. A diamon is an urge, a messenger, a divine thing inside each of us. In his book, *The Soul's Code*, James Hillman wrote very profoundly that each of us has a kind of diamon in us that is the song we're supposed to sing in our life, and that diamon cannot be over-identified with or ignored. If you over identify with the diamon, it will drive you crazy; if you ignore it, it becomes a demon. He gives examples of people, such as Judy Garland, who have over-identified with their diamons and gone crazy.

What I'm playing with here is this idea that we can expand our concept of Eros to realize that it is energy that creates, transforms and generates life. That's why Jung believed that Eros may be the kind of energy or power that creates new consciousness. On one level, we have Eros that is creating something new, and on another, we have its yoked opposite, *logos*, which brings the Eros into consciousness, and articulates and re-forms it. Eros needs *logos*, *logos* needs Eros, and we all need both *logos* and Eros. *Logos* is logic and words put in syntax to express thoughts; Eros creates *logos* and brings it into consciousness.

In terms of initiating and creating a relationship between two human beings, the purpose is then to bring something into being that has not been there before.

Like any force, Eros can be used either for creativity or for destruction, such as when we are overpowered by it. Not only does Eros initiate relationships or bring creative things into being, it also begins the process of people knowing each other. The longer I live, the older I get and the more experience I have, I'm more convinced that the word "known" is a synonym for love, an indication of how desperate we are to be known. And while the sum and substance of all relatedness may be the desire to be known, few of us have the resources or skills to be vulnerable enough to allow somebody to know us.

What is fairly clear is that if we're going to be vulnerable or intimate enough to be known, we need a container of some kind. That container can be a formal commitment, an informal history, or a professional relationship between therapist and patient; it can be formalized into a ritual process of sacrament like holy matrimony. Whatever the container, it must be able to handle the vulnerability and the energy. That's why when we are in the midst of Eros, we are, as French philosopher Pierre Teilhard de Chardin put it, playing with fire. And fire can transform; it can distill, it can burn away impurities, or it can destroy. So when Eros raises his and her head, be respectful. Honor the presence of this god.

In Hebrew, the word for knowing is *yada*. It means both to know and to have sexual intercourse. That's why you have to look at the context to see how it is being used. It's where the saying, "He knew her in the biblical sense" comes from, while the translation "He knew her not" means they didn't have sex. He knew her but he knew her not—here's the paradox.

Eros is the desire of a subject to be transformed through the relationship with another. Like every archetype, Eros has its dark side, which is destructive, rather than creative. But it's destructive in an interesting way because it puts the fire out by smothering it. The dark side of Eros is possessive, smothering or consuming. We find this incredible, dark paradox: We desire something so strongly we want to consume it, but if we consume it we no longer have it. In other words, we can't have our Eros and eat it, too.

It seems we are always in this sort of conflict. There's the possessive side—"I want this so desperately, I want it for my own, and I don't want anybody else to have it"—and the consuming one—"I don't want it to have a life apart from me." Where there is much creativity there is the potential for much destructiveness; as a result, the dark side of Eros can be very destructive. When Eros is loose and not conscious, it can consume or smother or possess something out of existence. That's why we need to honor and contain this mighty diamon.

What kind of container can best handle the numinous energy, the immense power of this form of love? Consciousness. In the face and presence of Eros, it is critical to be very conscious because the energy of Eros and its relationship to one's psyche is so stimulating and exciting that the ego wants to take it for itself. That's called inflation. If you are not highly conscious, that inflation becomes an infatuation and then an intoxication, which, in turn, spawns a lot of bad choices and bad decisions.

If you're going to play with fire—and make no mistake, Eros is fire—you must be very conscious and have a powerful container. I don't want to be overly dramatic, nor do I want to portray Eros as a something to be feared; it's just human love, but it can be a problem. Nearly all of the people who come and talk to me, almost without exception, have had problems with love, which tells me that love is a problem—and a common one.

Chapter 3
PHILIA: LOVE OF KINSHIP

BUT EROS ISN'T THE ONLY KIND OF LOVE. There is also Philia, the friendship kind of love or brotherly love of people who are together in a community, the smallest of which is a dyad, or a group of two. Friendship, that is, the love between two friends, may be the most undervalued kind of love in our culture. The very idea of not having a friend or a support system, of not having brothers and sisters who can hold our hand, be present with us in dark places and celebrate joyous occasions with us, is unthinkable. So Philia, or brotherly love like the city of Philadelphia, is the love that Jung called kinship libido.

Before you make any assumptions, libido, while most often associated in our culture with sexual drive, is really a synonym for energy; love, too, can be thought of as a synonym for energy. While Freud used libido specifically to describe sexual energy, Jung was quick to point out that the libido was really psychic energy and that referring to it as strictly sexual energy was to constrain and limit the understanding of it. If libido is psychic energy, then kinship libido is the kind of energy that makes us desire kin—not necessarily a family of origin, but a family of choice. There are men in my life, for example, whom I consider to be as much brothers to me as my biological brother. Likewise, I have no biological sisters, but there are women who are like sisters to me. This is crucial to understanding Philia, especially since little is written about friendship and the importance of companionship.

The word "companion" comes from the Latin *companis*, which means "with bread." A companion is someone with whom you break bread. But there's more to it than just ingesting and digesting bread. It's a relationship, a friendship, a sharing of food and thoughts and words with somebody who knows and cares about you. Sadly, as our society has become more mobile and we move more frequently from place to place, we occasionally wind up in a place where nobody knows us. And friendship isn't something that happens instantly; it takes a long time to get to know people and form relationships. The mystery of what creates attraction and complement and comfort in the presence of another is very complex.

Nevertheless, think about the hundreds of thousands of people who come in and out of our lives over a lifetime—how few of them know us and how few of them we want to know. That's why friendship is such a sacred thing. The two things most human beings find threatening are vulnerability and intimacy, and a good friend someone who is willing to know and be known. What we most desire is the thing we fear the most: We long to be longed for and we long to be known; we long to be intimate, but the idea of leaving ourselves open and vulnerable is terrifying. But vulnerability is necessary for intimacy because intimacy is self-disclosure in the face of one whose love and relationship you value.

On the other hand, self-disclosing to those you don't value is mere exhibitionism. Intimacy requires a container and some kind of commitment and consciousness. When you're intimate with another, you share fears, fantasies, feelings, failures, things that are important for another to know about you. Any person who doesn't know another, doesn't know herself, and any person who doesn't know herself, doesn't know another. Part of what Philia, or friendship, is about, is the mirroring that is necessary for us to know ourselves and be ourselves.

One of the things we say when we are in a complex is, "I just wasn't myself." Well, who the hell were you then? Not the person you were called to be. A friend will tell you the truth, that you're not being yourself. That kind of mirroring and individuation are very important and cannot be done in isolation. That's the paradox of Philia: I alone must become myself; I cannot become myself alone.

Agape is a different kind of relationship love. It is about the ability to empower another to be their authentic self. If Eros is the love that longs for, then Agape is the love that lets be. One of my mentors, John McQuarrie, who was the Lady Margaret professor of divinity at the University of Oxford and Canon Residentiary at Christ Church College, wrote in one of his books that "we should not refer to ourselves as human beings but as human becomings."

In his two-volume work titled Eros *and* Agape, Swedish theologian Anders Nygren goes to great lengths to make a distinction between Eros as a natural or human love and Agape as God's love. He linked the differences between them with two words for love; in classical Greek, the common word for love was Eros, which meant not only sexual love but also love of beauty and the desire for relatedness. Like Plato, Nygren even saw Eros as being a factor in the quest for God. But no matter how high a spiritual Eros might become, according to Nygren, it remains egocentric. Seeking to quell a longing and fill an emptiness, Eros is a limited and conditional love that demands reciprocity. Agape, on the other hand, is the truly selfless love of God, one he believes "is not a natural possibility for humans." He contends that Agape is not connected to Eros, that there is no path leading from Eros to Agape.

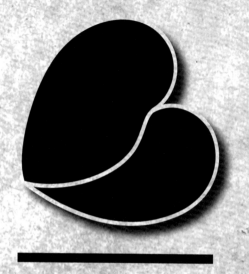

Chapter 4
AGAPE: LET IT BE

McQUARRIE, HOWEVER, DISAGREES. In his book *In Search of Humanity*, he helps us consider how Agape can be thought of in terms of human relations, pointing out that the stark division Nygren and others have made between natural love and Christian love is exaggerated, even mistaken. He goes further, asserting that Eros contains in itself the seed of Agape. While Nygren makes that point that much about Eros can be egocentric and demanding of reciprocity, McQuarrie believes not only that the beginning of Agape is within Eros, but also that the love that longs can be transferred into the love that lets be.

It's the idea of Agape—the love that lets be—that is most critical to analytical psychology. Love in its ontological sense is the study of being, so love in its sense of being is letting be.

McQuarrie develops this idea of letting be and expands on its importance in human individuation. Beyond our own individuation, any theological understanding of God's love must also include a sense of love that lets be; indeed, God's love is that he lets us be. That's why I get impatient with those who insist that God has a plan. In my mind, nothing could be further from the truth. The greatest love God can have for me is to not have a plan, but to let me be and become. That whole idea of an overarching divine plan is a simple ego defense against chaos; shit happens, and assuming that God has a hand in it helps to quell our anxiety.

When we talk of letting be, we must understand both parts: "letting" as empowering and "be" as enjoying the maximum range of being for any particular individual. In other words, letting be is a love that empowers and helps a person fully realize his potentiality for being, even if it runs counter to what we need or want him to be—a love that is self-sacrificing. McQuarrie sees this self-sacrificing love, or Agape, not only as love that allows another to become his or her own potential self, but also as a love that is, above all, the love of God towards his creation, humankind.

Agapeistic love is usually contrasted with Eros, and insofar as Eros contains any self-centeredness, this contrast is justified. According to McQuarrie's examinations in *In Search of Humanity*, these two apparently opposing forms of love are ultimately not so different. As one passes into the other, we have an instance of the so-called natural becoming perfected, or perhaps transformed, by grace. In the modern world, erotic love has been arbitrarily narrowed to mean sexual passion. But in truth, erotic love manifests itself at its highest in the longing for God, which contains in it the seed of Agape. If our longing is fulfilled not by effort but by grace, then love that longs is transformed into the love that lets be or empowers another to be. It's important here to note that this empowering love is not about tolerating self-destructive behavior, abuse or abandonment; sometimes the healthiest thing we can do to empower somebody to be their truest self is to not be in a relationship with them.

When we connect to another human being at that level, we are also connecting with the transcendent or the holy in them; through that connection, we empower them to be the truest selves they can be. In addition, if we can work our way through the spider webs of complexes and projections, we might occasionally experience the divine in human love, and that's Agape.

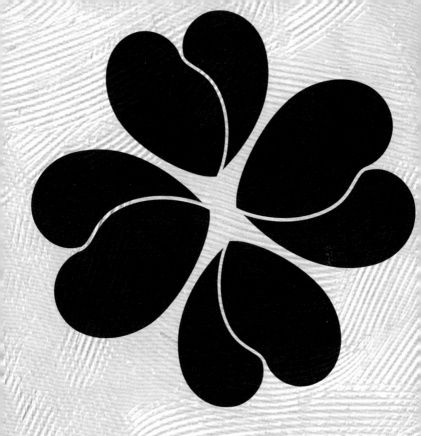

Chapter 5

THE ARCHETYPES
OF LOVE

W HEN CONSIDERING THE mystery of love and the overwhelming nature of it, I think it's safe to say that angels rush in where fools fear to tread. Why reverse the traditional saying? Because fools are out talking about obvious things, simplistic things that are anti-intellectual; angels are messengers trying to discern something of the truth in this human journey, so they rush in.

In his autobiography, *Memories, Dreams, Reflections*, C.G. Jung offers this profound summary and intro- duction to the concept of love in a section titled "Late Thoughts:"

At this point the fact forces itself on my attention that beside the field of reflection there is another equally broad, if not broader, area in which rational understanding and rational modes of representation find scarcely anything they are able to grasp. This is the realm of Eros. In classical times, when such things were properly understood, Eros was considered a god whose divinity transcended in our human limits, and who therefore could neither be comprehended nor represented in any way. I might, as many before me have attempted to do, venture an approach to this daimon, whose range of activity extends from the endless spaces of heavens to the dark abyss of hell; but I falter before the task of finding the language, which might adequately express the incalculable paradoxes of love.

Eros is a *kosmogonos*, a creator and father-mother of all higher consciousness. I sometimes feel that Paul's words—"Though I speak with the tongues of men and of angels, and have not love"—might well be the first condition of all cognition and the quintessence of divinity itself. Whatever the learned interpretation may be of the sentence, "God is love," the words affirm the *complexio oppositorum* [union of opposites] of the Godhead. In my medical experience as well as in my own life I have again and again been faced with the mystery of love, and have never been able to explain what it is. Like Job, I had to "lay my hand on my mouth, I have spoken once and I will not answer." Here is the greatest and the smallest, the remotest and the nearest, the highest and the lowest, and we cannot discuss one side of it without also discussing the other. No language is adequate to this paradox. Whatever one can say, no words express the whole. To speak of partial aspects is always too much or too little, for only the whole is meaningful. "Love bears all things" and "endures all things" (1Cor. 13:7) These words say all that is to be said; nothing can be added to them.

For we are in the deepest sense the victims and instruments of cosmogonic "love." I put the word in quotations marks to indicate that I do not use it in its connotations of desiring, preferring, favoring, wishing, and similar feelings, but as something superior to the individual, a unified and undivided whole. Being a part, man cannot grasp the whole. He is at its mercy. He may ascent to it or rebel against it; but he is always caught up by it and enclosed within it. He is dependent upon it and sustained by it. Love is his light and his darkness, whose end he cannot see. "Love ceases not"—whether he speaks with the "tongues of angels" or with scientific exactitude traces the life of the cell down to its uttermost source. Man can try to name love, showering upon it all the names at his command, and he still will be involved in endless self-deceptions. If he possesses a grain of wisdom, he will lay down his arms and name the unknown by the more unknown, *ignotum per ignotius*—that is, by the name of God. This is a confession of his subjection, his imperfection, and his dependence, but at the same time a testimony to his freedom to choose between truth and error.

In those paragraphs, Jung sets for us as a backdrop the impossibility of the task of comprehending this paradox of paradoxes: the idea of love. Let me follow that up by again offering the quotation from Teilhard de Chardin: "After we have mastered the winds, the waves, the tides and gravity, we shall harness for God the energies of love. Then for the second time in the history of the world we will have discovered fire." Where does this lead us? To our starting point: the idea that love is a life force, an energy. Not surprisingly, fire is a good analogy for love; it is transforming agent that can be simultaneously creative and destructive, depending on the conduit for the heat. If love is too loose in relationship, it needs a conduit, and perhaps that conduit is consciousness.

It's possible that consciousness can be used for transformation and creativity, rather than for destruction. But since consciousness is such a powerful force with so much energy that it may not be able to conduct love. As Teilhard de Chardin wrote, "Driven by the forces of love, the fragments of the world seek each other so that the world may come to being." One of the things occurring is here is the archetype of love; that life force, the potentially transforming and creative energy, is the glue that holds these fragments together to make a whole. By being as conscious as we can about this singularly human phenomena, we may be able to harness love and use it as a resource for wholeness. Love can be the energy that, like glue, pulls together the disparate parts of organisms, both intra-personally and inter-personally, in the vertical relationship we have with ourselves and in the horizontal relationships we have with others.

That leads us to the four primary relationships of love that most of us experience in our life's journey: mother, father, others and self. We have already looked at Eros, Philia and Agape, the three kinds of love. Eros is the life force that harbors the longing to connect, relate and create, and the impulse for creative ideas and expression. We have Eros for others, for objects as well as subjects. In addition, Eros has a limited ability to sustain the energy of attraction or desire—once we possess something we desire, we no longer desire it. The dark side of that is an insidious destructive pattern of consumption or possession.

Philia, the brotherly or sisterly love or the love of friendship, is one of the most undervalued relationships in the human experience. As poet and essayist Philip Lopate says, friendship is a long conversation. Friends are those who can be guides, mentors, companions or mirrors. While I alone must become myself, I depend on others to tell me things about myself that I don't know, and to help me know myself in a way I couldn't otherwise, through reflection and mirroring. In the end, friendship is a long conversation is about getting to know you.

Getting to know someone means that you allow yourself to be intimate. My definition of intimacy is self-disclosure in the face of someone you value. As I have said, self-disclosure in the face of somebody you don't know is simply exhibitionism; intimacy, on the other hand, is a very sacred, private and modest thing. The friendship love of Philia can also lead to Eros, which is a part of friendship; sometimes friends can have Eros for one another. I believe we can have homoerotic relationships that are not homosexual relationships—it just means that we want to connect with or relate to somebody of the same gender. We can be friends with somebody, and then suddenly have this desire to know them in another way. When friendship moves from Philia to Eros, sometimes the friendship gets lost, because the love of another is very complicated. Without being overly cynical, many a good friendship has been ruined by marriage. We bring everything we have, including all our own baggage, into a relationship, and for most of us, there are many baggage cars on that train.

Although Eros is the love that longs for, it also contains within it the seed of Agape, the love that lets be. That is, letting be not in the sense of being apathetic, but in the sense of empowering one to be one's most authentic Self. Agape means that I want my life force to empower you to be as true to your authentic Self as you can be, given the limitations of our fate. We do not, after all, have control over everything. But control is an illusion we need; it's one of those defenses the ego uses against anxiety and the unpredictability of life. In fact, we have very limited control over how we react and respond to things. In a way, then, Agape is the love that doesn't try to control, but rather allows things to unfold and empowers the unfolding of the beauty of one's truth. This is just one framework for thinking about love. The very thing we can't talk about seems to be that very thing we want to talk about.

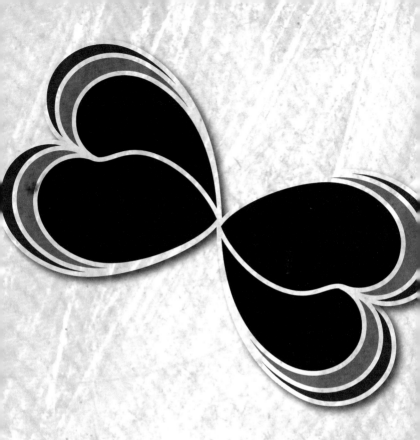

Chapter 6

MOTHER LOVE

FROM THIS GENERAL understanding of love, let's move to the first large archetypal love that we experience: the love of the mother, or the lack thereof. "Mother" is an archetype, and by that we mean that every human being has exactly the same need for longing for and desire for mother.

Archetypes are the predisposed patterns of human behavior. They are to the psyche what instincts are to the soma, soma, in this context meaning "body." It's as if the human psyche is imprinted with a kind of unconscious longing to experience certain things in its journey, and one of them is mother love. So we are born looking instinctively for an experience of the mother, regardless of our birthplace, gender or ethnic origin. Gender may have some influence on the way mothers do or do not connect with us, but the longing is the same for all of us.

The archetype of mother is a psychological principal, but it is not gender-specific. By this definition, men can also mother. In his book *Iron John: A Book About Men,* Robert Bly talks about how the world needs more male mothers. Woman can father, and I think in a healthy way what the world needs is more female fathers. In simple terms, father is about order, power, and doing, and the mother is about nurture, and being. We come into the world longing for, needing the experience of mother. In addition to the archetypal mother, there is our experience of mother. This is where everyone is different. Your experience of a mother is different from mine, and your need for a mother and your experience of her begins to define of your personality. That leads us to the third mother, the inner mother, which is the mother complex. The relationship between our archetypal need for a mother and our experience with our biological mother and surrogate mothers sets up for us what kind of a mother we have on the interior. The kind of mother we carry with us—the kind of inner complex we have that is a part of our unconscious personality—is the mother complex.

Like any other love relationship, mother love contains the previously mentioned three kinds of love: Eros, Philia and Agape. The longing to connect, relate and create also seems to be a very maternal kind of love. What is more creative than the creation of another human being? What is more loving than creating something? Most of us are here, after all, because of an attempt at Eros. Our parents, whoever they are, made love or attempted to make love, which began our human journey. Then there is the kind of mother love that arises from the mere fact that our mother gestated us, gave birth to us, and brought us into being. And ultimately begins the kind of love that we call nurturing love, the part of Eros that is the connecting and relating and continuing to create.

The mother-child, mother-infant dyad begins at conception, but it doesn't end at birth. It adapts as the people involved change; we have a symbiotic system that can last two years or forty or seventy-five. The symbiosis doesn't always have an end date. Even if the mother dies, our relationship to her doesn't end. Even her death sets up a kind of mother that we carry in our unconscious, which is the mother complex. I talk to people every day about their mother, and if their mother has been deceased for twenty years, we're not really talking about the woman who gave birth to them, we are talking about the mother complex—the mobile mother.

In an ideal world, the mother provides the infant and the child with several qualities of love that are important for healthy development. The first would be containment; it is a simple continuation of containment of the womb. Our first experience of mother is the security and safety of a womb. I one time heard a woman describe that when she was carrying her children, she felt like a Brink's truck with wonderful gold inside. That containment, that sense of making an organism feel contained and protected from the very beginning, does not end with the actual birth; it must continue. I love to watch my daughters-in-law swaddle my grandchildren. The tightly wrapped blanket is a continuation of the womb containment. We describe our office and relationships with our analysands, as the "analytic container." And if containment continues as a loving form, then as we age, we still feel that sense of safety and security. It's an interesting, very Agapeistic love because it empowers us to be.

In addition to containment, we need literal nurture—not just food but nourishment. With mother's milk comes the mother's attitude toward the infant—that is psychological milk. In fact, the attitude the mother has is the attitude the child takes toward herself. The child doesn't know the difference at that point between herself and her mother, so her mother is herself. Once again, the hope is that the inability to distinguish between Self and mother fades, but sometimes it doesn't.

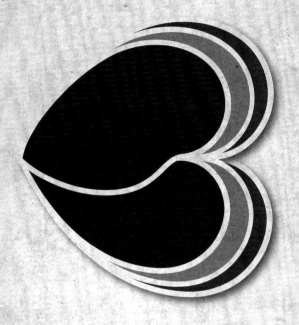

Chapter 7

TOO MUCH OR
NOT ENOUGH?

A MOTHER'S ATTITUDE TOWARD her child at the earliest stage of development has a huge influence on the identity or the attitude the child eventually has about herself, her environment and the world. So the mother's attitude must be able to appropriately answer such fundamental questions as, "Is this a safe place? Am I valued? Do I belong?" I have been—and still am—asking those questions all my life. The deprivation of a healthy attitude sets up the kind of neurotic adjustment to relationship with one's self and the relationship with one's environment. A mother's love for her child has a great deal to do with the way the child's personality develops.

According to Jung, there are only two kinds of mothers, too much or not enough. Too much mothering is what we have talked about as the dark side of Eros, the possessiveness and the consumption. A negative mother is the mother who is unable to create an attitude of containment and nourishing psychological milk that affirms and values. There are a variety of reasons for which she might be unable to do that. Some mothers haven't been mothered themselves and, as such, have had no mother on which to model their own behavior. Some are wounded in some physical way; still others are narcissistic or addicted, and so on.

Jung refers to the negative mother and her message, which is "I will love you if you will please me" or, more subtly, "I will love you if you continue to be an extension of me." A child who receives that message grows up believing that her worth is directly proportionate to her ability to please. It's a simple, but powerful, rubric: "I will love you if you please me." The child who grows up with that message becomes gifted in her ability to please. She adapts and conforms; she dances as fast as she can in order to achieve that pleasure, that delight she is seeking. Here is a glimpse at the psychology of love and the flicker of understanding that love has a great deal to do with psychic development and the development of personality. The primary love of the mother—of lack of it—is the first experience we have of love.

No discussion about the role of the mother is complete without also discussing the role of the father. In terms of his presence, the father is extremely important to the child's ability to separate from the mother. One of the classical symbols of the masculine power is the sword; a good, healthy place for the sword to be placed is on the psychological umbilical cord. The father can provide that kind of power and energy. As I've said so often, the message of the mother is, "You can't live without me, but if you stay here I'll kill you." That's what we call a conflict. And while it may not be literally true, there is truth to it; the dark side of the mother is to possess and consume and keep you dependent. In some way, I believe that all our mothers gave us a message at some point about how angry they were at us for growing up.

The love of a mother, if it is in the realm of mental health, must have Agape. In this case, the mother's love is of such quality that she is willing to get out of the way in order that her child may become the person she is intended to be. The love that lets be isn't the love that longs or possesses; it's the love that empowers. In addition, there is the empowerment of the father, who takes the child from the mother and shows her how to be human. This contrast of doing and being is very important. As humans, we need both. Agape, as we're framing it, is essential in terms of the mother love that allows and empowers her child to leave. In reframing Agape, McQuarrie took it a step further, explaining that it wasn't just the love of God, but its very divinity that allows us to treat one another as God treats us.

These days, I find myself in a dynamic theological place, and I think that's the best place to be, I don't particularly believe in any anthropomorphic images, such as God as mother or God as father, because it infantilizes us to keep looking at God as a parent. The church has done that. If I had any anthropomorphic image of God right now, it would not be as mother or father; rather it would be as lover, in much the same way the Sufis refer to God as the Beloved. God is not a concept or an image, but an experience. If we experience Agape with another, we have experienced God, because God is love and those who dwell in love, dwell in God. Whether it is with our father, mother, a significant other or a friend, if we have that experience of Agape then we have had an experience of the divine or the transcendent.

On a more earthly plain, the longing for a mother is one of the strongest we, as humans, ever have. In my mind, we try to make a mother out of virtually anything that will nurture us or offer us security—the church, our university alma mater, even corporations (remember "Ma Bell?"). It's a strong archetypal need, so we are always looking for somebody to mother us. Where things can get complicated is when what we refer to as love is an unconscious, archetypal longing or need. That's not love; rather, it is a neurotic longing that we are acting out under the guise of love. Some men, for example, try to make their wife into a mother and vice versa. The baggage we bring into our relationships—the unfulfilled needs in our primary love relationships—can get in the way of Eros.

That brings me back to consciousness as the conduit for a healthy love relationship. It is important for us to recognize and take responsibility for what remains unfinished in our primary relationship and whether we are using our current relationship to heal the past one. Ultimately this is what psychotherapy or psychoanalysis is about: trying to discern what, in my earliest development, has impeded my healthy development as an adult. Where we experience that most dramatically is in our attempts at love. The love of a mother for a child is very definitive in much of our later relationships. In simple terms, if we had a good enough mother we will have good enough relationships with ourselves and others; if we didn't, then we have reparation to do in the second half of life.

Chapter 8
FATHER LOVE

THE ABILITY TO NURTURE is not gender-specific; it doesn't necessarily come coded into the DNA. While there are plenty of mothers who can give their children the love they need, empowering them to become healthy human beings, there are those who cannot. By the same token, there are many nurturing fathers who are capable of being both mother and father. A single human being can mother and father, and many single parents are called to do this very difficult task. I know many men who are very nurturing and many women who are very discerning in providing that kind of energy that child needs to separate from home. Quite often in an analytic process, people will experience the profound realization that their mother was their father, and their father was their mother.

What is father love? What is the love of a father for a child? Interestingly enough, the general statement from analytical psychology about the energy of the father and mother archetype has to do with nurture and power: mother nurturer and father power. In this case, the father power is the kind focused on separation and discernment, on civilization or civilizing. The father's foremost responsibility in love is to allow the child to separate from the mother through the relationship with the father. Realizing that from gestation through age two, for example, there has been a literal and psychological symbiosis between the child and mother, it is very important that the father is there to offer a separating kind of love so that child can begin the separation process from mother. The father's first role in a child's life is to provide a separating energy that says essentially, "Let me show you a world that you can live in without mother," and "I will empower you to live in that world with confidence and competence."

The classical symbols of the masculine or phallic energy are the sword and the lance. The sword is that separating function, a figurative cutting of the umbilical cord. The two greatest separation points in a child's life are ages two and fourteen, so fourteen is really just a recreation of two. My own son came to me one day when he was fourteen and said he wanted to talk to me. He'd had a horrible nightmare the night before, so horrible that he almost didn't want to tell me. I told him I could handle it and encouraged him to go on. What he dreamed was that he had beaten his mother to death with a baseball bat. My response was, "That's a great dream, son."

I didn't want to appear overly enthusiastic. But I think a moment later it became thoroughly transparent to him that, psychologically, he was an ambivalent fourteen-year-old wondering whether or not he was going to be able to separate from his mother. This is where the father comes, the father who can show that fourteen-year-old a world he can live in without her and empower him to become independent. There is no greater love a father can have for his child than to help his child outgrow him. In the Christian scriptures, Jesus says to his disciples "You will do far greater things then those which I have done." Now that's a good father.

The negative father, on the other hand, is the father who does not want his child to exceed. So if we are talking about love in this sense of empowerment, we mean love that empowers a child to become independent, to have a sense of competence and confidence. A father can literally assume the role of teacher when, for example, he shows his child how to start a lawn mower, how to run a computer, how to check the well or change a tire. Not surprisingly then, it's valuable for a father to be involved very early on with the child, so that the child knows he has an advocate, and that his advocate is championing his independence, competence, confidence, mastery and success. Most of the message passed from father to child is based on what the father models—what he does, not what he says. Does the father live his life in a confident and competent way? Is he available so the child can see what it means to be confident and competent person?

Chapter 9
THE FATHER–
DAUGHTER DYNAMIC

THE DYNAMIC BETWEEN father and daughter is a bit different, just as it is between son and mother. With a daughter and mother, the daughter has to do her separating, but she doesn't have to be different from mother. A little boy, on the other hand, not only has to separate, he must also not be like her; he has to be like a male. That's why, boys with absentee fathers often separate from their mothers through violence. That is the dark side of the father, and the violence can primarily manifest in attitudes toward women. I believe every man harbors a little fear of the feminine, an ambivalence about whether we can trust the feminine. That's why our culture is replete with misogynistic attitudes and acts of violence toward women, because of the lack of presence or modeling of what it means to be a healthy man.

The father with the daughter needs to empower her just the way he empowers the son. A good example of a classical archetypal story about how a father can impair the daughter is *The Handless Maiden,* a folktale in which the father literally cuts a pact with the devil to have his daughter's hands cut off. Literally, she is not able to handle the world. The healthy father is one who teaches his daughter how to handle the world, rather than assuming that the daughter, being a girl, doesn't need to be taught how to be independent and competent in the world, the way boys do. I have heard so many stories in my practice, both as a priest and an analyst, from women whose fathers so devalued and dishonored them that they have carried an incredible father wound and father hunger with them throughout their lives. The negative father, instead of empowering the child with competence and confidence, leaves the child feeling impotent or inferior.

If the healthy father empowers, then the dark father overpowers or abuses. Why would a man violently abuse a child? Why would he overpower a helpless victim? Because *he* is impotent, and impotent males overpower helpless people. The little girl who feels helpless is the handless maiden; if the daughter receives too much father energy or too much father attention, the problem becomes one of daddy's little girl, the eternal adolescent or the seductive hysteric, who is so much the center of her father's attention that she never moves beyond it.

She spends her life either seeking it over and over again or in some reaction against it. If the father is not present often enough, she spends her life looking for something that will assuage her father hunger. She may even idealize him.

With the son, the father who empowers teaches his son to be competent and confident in the world, and to become more fully himself than the father was able to accomplish. That father is not threatened by the child's success; he delights in it. But impotent males are threatened by anybody who might exceed or succeed them, so the son is either empowered, or overpowered through aggression. If the father doesn't have enough incumbent health of his own to balance between his masculine/feminine functions, the imbalance can result in too much power and be very wounding toward the child.

What the daughter wants is affection without sexuality. I have a female psychoanalyst friend who says every little girl wants her daddy to adore her and say "I love you. You don't ever have to worry. I'll be the gatekeeper, and I'll never have sex with you." It's not about saying those words literally but about setting a clear boundary and knowing the difference between affection and sexuality. We are so cut off from our bodies that we don't really understand or appreciate the wonder and beauty of human sexuality. If a man finds himself sexually stimulated through affection, it scares the hell out of him. He runs away rather than celebrating that stimulation as a natural part of being human.

How can a man be affectionate with a little child and not be sexually stimulated? And how in the world can he be unconscious enough to ruin the child's psychosexual development by acting on that stimulation? All relationships are sexual—how can we be in a relationship that's not sexual? How can we not be sexually stimulated in relationships even with our children? But there is a tremendous difference between a thought and a thought acted upon. Many father-daughter relationships change overnight once the daughter reaches puberty, and the little girl never gets over it or understands it.

Children are incredible observers and lousy interpreters. Because they are so pre-verbal and non-verbal for the most of their early development, they don't miss a thing. They see everything, they observe it all, but they don't understand any of it. In a form of early narcissism, they think it's all about them. If Daddy disappears, it's because he doesn't love me anymore because I'm not attractive. It's the father responsibility to be healthy and mature enough to love the daughter and, at the same time, let her be very confident that he's in charge of the boundaries in the relationship.

In addition to the separation and the empowerment, there is another important form of love from the father archetype: it is discipline, or civilizing. The patriarchy sets boundaries and rules for normative behavior, and in the culture; it creates codes and laws so that we can learn to live within civilization. This is a critical function of the archetypal father—without it, the species doesn't survive. I may have a liberal viewpoint about the world, but I believe in laws. I also believe that Jesus taught me to recognize when the law is appropriate and when it is a barrier against individuation or health. In the gospel of St. Thomas, for example, Jesus is walking around and he sees a group of men plucking grain on the Sabbath, even though it's against the law to work on that holy day. So he says to them very wisely, "Man! If thou knowest what thou doest, thou art blessed. But if thou knowest not, thou art cursed and a transgressor of the Law." In other words, if you are going to break the law do it consciously, do it because you have a higher value or a higher calling.

As a young priest in the early 1970s, I spent many hours saying that very thing to young men about Vietnam: You can break this law if you have a higher calling, but you will pay for it and you are going to have to do it consciously. The same was true when my son, Pittman, had an emergency appendectomy. I believe in stop signs, and I wouldn't want to live in a culture that didn't have them; I am also a pretty conservative driver. But the night he had to have emergency surgery, I ran every stop sign between my house and the hospital. In other words, I had a higher calling than that particular law.

It's an issue of discernment: discernment about civilization and law, and learning that discipline is about setting boundaries with love. Not long ago, a woman told me that her kids hate her, that they think she doesn't love them because every night it is a struggle to get them to eat, bathe and go to bed and keep them from fighting with each other. My response to her was simple: "They know you love them because you do discipline them." Discipline is, after all, a form of love.

My entire adult life, I have been listening to people say over and over that their parents didn't love them because they never set any limits, never had any expectations and didn't seem to care. One woman I know, whose mother was a divorced alcoholic who didn't set any limits, would go out in the evening with her friends and tell them that she had to be home by midnight or her mother would "kill her." She so wanted that love of discipline and of setting out rules for normative behavior that she invented a responsible parent to impose it.

That's not to say that women can't offer the discipline of love just as well as men. Women can father, and men can mother. But we're are talking about the father archetype here, about the importance of the father's voice and availability to say "no." Traditionally, the voice of the feminine is "yes" and the voice of the masculine is "no." Both are important. As I have often said, where would we be if Eve and Mary hadn't said yes to those outlandish temptations? Eve said "yes" and agreed to pay the price for consciousness; Mary agreed to house the son of God. That's the voice of the feminine "yes," while the voice of the masculine is limits and boundaries and "no." Just as we need both salt and pepper, we need a balance of the feminine and masculine voices. Without balance, there is either too much aggression or too much chaos.

In his book, *Finding Our Fathers*, author and psychologist Samuel Osherson wrote that only seventeen percent of the people he surveyed felt they had a healthy relationship with their father. Why is that? We have lived for so long in a patriarchal society that we've all been robbed of anything feminine in us, particularly men. Our relationships with our fathers are difficult because they have traditionally been lopsidedly masculine. And our fathers may know about *logos*, but they don't know much about Eros. That means they don't know how to be in the feminine function of relatedness, creativity, connectedness; they don't necessarily know how to mother, that is to gestate and contain. In the 1950s and early 1960s, the message I received as a male was yield to all authority, conform and don't feel. Sprinkled in there was of the message of compete and defeat.

Another reason there has been such dissatisfaction with the father relationship is that many fathers simply haven't been there. This is Robert Bly's primary thesis in *Iron John: A Book About Men*. After the Industrial Revolution, fathers left the farms where they were available to the children and went to work in the factories. Add to that the pressure on men to compete and defeat, be the breadwinner and the hunter, and you have big problems for males in our culture.

While it's easy to lapse into saying that men father and women mother, I try to avoid the stereotypical idea that men are this way and women are that way. In a lecture at the Houston Jung Center several years ago, pioneering Jungian analyst Marion Woodman said, "The greatest threat to the feminine principal in our culture is the patriarchal female." It takes a sophisticated consciousness to realize that not all men are alike and all women are not alike.

Chapter 10

DISCERNING THE MYSTERY

AS HUMANS, WE FAIL AT LOVE because we don't really have enough consciousness about what it is—and, just as importantly, what it isn't. Many times we understand something by looking at its opposite, much as looking at disgrace opened up the concept of grace. When we understand what love isn't, it becomes clearer to us then what love is. As we have tried to comprehend the difference between neurosis and pathology and love and discovered there are some areas in which they overlap, we have also discovered just how difficult it is to discern this mystery called love. And it is a mystery; according to Jung, it is the greatest mystery, a paradoxical concept and construct. We have a tentative framework of Eros, Philia, and Agape as a place to begin our journey toward consciousness about this mystery.

The love of another, is a multi-dimensional phenomenon, a human experience with myriad aspects and complications. Many of the words we use to refer to concepts, such as love, truth or beauty, are merely symbols that point to a mystery. Therefore simple *logos*, logic or reason isn't enough to discern such experience. However, there are several things going on in this attraction to an "other," or what our culture would call the "significant other." One of the functions or purpose of the other is to help us know ourselves. I would like to be able to dismiss, as so many Jungians do, the idea of romantic love. I suspect that, in addition to Jungian analysts, many mental health professionals and, indeed, most human beings are suspicious of romantic love by now.

I haven't quite given up on romantic love, but I understand its limitations and I feel as though it is integral to the process of true love. When I refer to romantic love, I mean the kind of love that inflates and infatuates us. In that experience, we have the opportunity to deepen the love through the trauma of the projection collapsing, or the inflation deflating. Through that suffering, we begin to experience the truth and depth of love, or true love.

Basic analytical psychology says that the attraction to a significant other is really the projection of some aspect of yourself onto them. The significant other carries the anima or an animus projection, and that initiates a relationship, which causes an obsession and eventually an inflation or infatuation with that person. Inevitably, the infatuation creates a fall—that's why we call it falling in love—and the projection collapses. What you are left with is another person, a real live human being with whom you must figure out how to grow in love together or help each other become the fullest possible people you were meant to be. Sounds like Agape, the love that lets be.

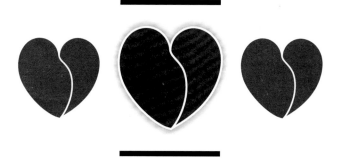

In Robert Johnson's book, *We,* he concludes that romantic love has become a substitute for spirituality in Western culture. In the realm of romantic love, we tend to talk about the immature, initial attraction, which must mature or it will end. It must expand into higher consciousness, into something deeper than simply the intoxication of the initial falling in love. Romantic idealism is another aspect of the love that many of us cling to: the idea that the other will complete us, and bring meaning to our lives, that this person carries within him or her the possibility of allowing me to feel complete. Polly Young-Eisendrath calls this the dream lover, the one we have dreamed of, the one who will rescue me from my inauthenticity and escort me into the holy. It is both projection and the expectation that this person is not only a god or goddess, but also that he or she this person will help heal, fix and transform us. The attraction is to help us mature; with the experience of having loved and lost comes the possibility of maturation.

There is, of course, the biology of love: the need for incarnation, the need for the soul to have location and experience through a physical body. Eighteenth-century Romantic poet William Blake wrote that the senses are the inlets of the soul. So our sensorium provides us not only with great resources for the experience of another, but also for the experience of the divine. Therein, you have the two primary opportunities in a love relationship: the opportunity to know and be known with an other and the opportunity to experience the transcendent.

As I'm fond of saying, I have never had a soul come into my office without a body. We are not dualistic about body and soul, but we are body *and* soul. Our body not only locates and identifies soul, but it is also the inlet for the experience of soul senses: taste, touch, sight, sound and smell. Sexuality is an important vehicle for knowing and being known, and most of us know that touch maybe one of the most primary healing resources available to us. Bodywork is about healing, and touch is about healing. Indeed, the largest organ we have is our skin; the idea of God being reincarnated with skin on him is a part of this understanding of the other and what the other might be able to do for us. But there is no magic other—we just have human beings to project onto. So when the projections collapse, we feel as though we missed something or lost something, when in fact we have an opportunity to gain something.

To know and to be known is one of the functions of the other, and one of the ways we know the other is through that power of presence. That power brings us to a much spiritual or theological understanding of the significant other, that he or she may be an incarnation of the transcendent. Perhaps this seems grandiose, but incarnation is not an exclusively Christian concept. It simply means the experience of the transcendent in something tangible. For example, a significant love between people who are committed to experiencing something creative and transforming in a relationship provides an opportunity to experience the transcendent. That's why in the Christian scriptures John wrote that "God is love," further making the point by saying that that those who dwell in love dwell in God and God in them. This gives us a theological basis for the idea that love is not something necessarily narcissistic or selfish, but rather an opportunity for experiencing the transcendent or the divine.

Chapter 11
EGO VERSUS SELF

A HUMAN RELATIONSHIP PUTS into play all kinds of possibilities—some of them destructive, some neurotic and some pathological—so it is very difficult for us to love and be loved. In my opinion, a human relationship is not about a magical other that one spends one's entire life trying to discover; instead, it is much more about two highly conscious people, who discover through their conversation that there is something greater than either of them.

When we talk about love or Agape, we aren't referring to the dark side of Eros or the dark side of mother love. We are talking about the ability to be conscious, that through a relationship we will know and be known in a way we have never before experienced, and that we are committed to going as deeply as possible into that knowing. What's more, we will go into that sacred space, bring all our baggage with us and pray for the ability to see that baggage as enrichment for the relationship. Actually, I think many times our relationships are our vehicles for growing up. On the one hand, it is about being known and knowing, which helps us grow up; on the other hand, it is about seeking the mysterious divine in a mundane event and experiencing the extraordinary in an ordinary human relationship.

I wrote a poem about human relationships, which is titled "No, Known," Here is an excerpt appropriate to the topic we're exploring:

And so I've been curious,
about the sounds of no and known.

So much of life has been centered around the no,
Setting the boundary and barrier,
Living the ethic. Making the decide:
You know, suicide, homicide.

But, now to be known.
The conditions are different.

To be known with the leaves
blowing their own way.
To be known like the shine of dew
on a new day's lawn.
To be known in the fullest, the deepest
and the longing.

This is where things are in soft focus.
Where nothing is eroded.
The more it is seen the more it grows.

I would be happy at this time to be known
Where the bones are,
Where the meaning is,
Where the deepest curves of the body's map
lead to a new geography.

To be known.
To never say no again.

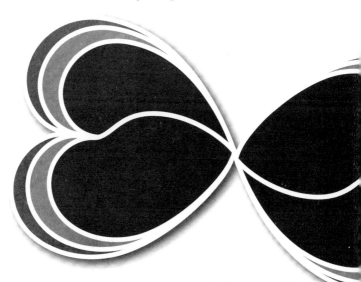

The ending may be poetic hyperbole, but it really means never to say "no" to being known. Throughout much of our lives, we have been heavily dependent on not being known, and to never again say "no" to the opportunity of knowing another and being known by another is one of the significant opportunities and resources love can bring us. The other opportunity is the experience of the divine or the transcendent. If one sense, if we are in the face of the letting be love of Agape, that's the kind of love that transforms and carries with it significant meaning. When we are committed to that kind of love, we get much closer to understanding and experiencing whatever we mean by the love of God. In Jungian terms, it is the love of one Self for a Self in another. Such love gets the ego out of the way.

Ego is about attachment, structure, survival and self-gratification; the Self is about giving up or letting go in order to be a part of the whole. The Self is the *imago Dei*, or the image of God, in every human being, and this kind of love with another is the attempt to experience *imago Dei* in that person. If that happens, it is a transforming experience that brings meaning to the whole enterprise. It is worthwhile to experience the love of a Self for a Self where the ego is out of the way. Once that happens, we can talk about God as love.

As level of the love of an other is about experiencing the Self, so must the Self realize that it is not about romantic idealism. Rather, it is about the rigorous, vigorous, acceptance of the totality of another and the vulnerability of openness to knowing and being known by another. Through that, we move to the personal. Carl Rogers, who was among the pioneers of psychotherapy research, said, "that which is most personal is most universal;" I am saying that which is most personal is transpersonal. What does that mean? In a significant personal relationship with another, we move through the personal into the transpersonal. That's why the world is better for this—people struggling to love one another in healthy ways benefits the whole.

Ultimately, through the love of another, we realize, in a trickster kind of way, that the other that we have sought for so long is ourselves. In other words, a significant relationship with an other will introduce us to ourselves. The Sufis have a wonderful saying, "I beheld myself, I loved myself, I inseminated myself, I gestated myself and I birthed myself." It is through another that we are able to finally begin to have an authentic relationship with ourselves. That's not so easy. We haven't had much encouragement in our culture for loving ourselves. I grew up in a tradition that said we were miserable sinners. Most systems, in fact, do not promote self-love because of the misunderstanding of narcissism, egocentricity, egoism, inflation and grandiosity that comes through the reaction formation to one who doesn't love oneself. If one truly loves oneself, the first thing one does is get grounded, not inflated. We just don't have much encouragement or modeling for loving ourselves.

Chapter 12
SELF-COMPASSION

WHEN I RAISE THAT possibility with people, they don't even know what I am talking about. We all have dissociative identity disorders in which we have different personalities that we carry around with us; we have different voices in us, and many of them are what Jungians call "complexes" These complexes have core beliefs, one of which is that we are no damn good. The only antidote for that shadow is love. We must love all of those parts of ourselves, but first we have to know them. If another is able to love those desperate parts of ourselves, then perhaps we can both know ourselves and love ourselves. Love can cast out fear, love can quiet the voice of judgment that never stops talking inside us.

Part of this thing about loving one's self is what the

Buddhists call "self-compassion."

Based on the work of University of Texas researcher Kristin Neff, Ph.D., compassion occurs when you are touched by the suffering of another, when you let somebody else's pain into your heart rather than ignoring it or avoiding it. When this occurs, feelings of kindness and caring for the other person's welfare spontaneously arise. When we experience compassion for , made a mistake or performed a misdeed, it means that we have taken an open-minded, non-judgmental attitude toward that person, instead of an attitude of harsh criticism or severe judgments. Another unique feature of compassion is that ability to recognize one's shared humanity with another. When we see someone who has failed or is suffering, rather than be grateful that it's not our problem, we suffer with them.

Self-compassion requires us to be touched by our own suffering. Rather than ignore or repress our own pain, we stop and realize the difficulty and hardship of it. It also means that we desire well-being for ourselves and feel compelled to help heal our own pain. And when we fail or make mistakes, we have a kind, understanding attitude toward ourselves that accepts our limitations and imperfections instead of harshly judging.

Ultimately, we see our personal experience in the light of the common human experience. Instead of feeling isolated and separated when we fail or are suffering, we stop to realize that many others feel what we are feeling, that it's just part of being human.

With regard to love of the other, this means we are talking about ourselves as the other. We need to love and have compassion for ourselves, just as we would for any other human being. Why would we have double standards? We are loving, forgiving, accepting of others—why can we not do that for ourselves? When we talk about loving the other, we must include ourselves as being the most important significant other we could ever love. The only relationship you will go to the grave with is the one you have with yourself; it would be good mental hygiene to work on improving that relationship and developing this self-compassion. It may be both the most healthy mental hygene and deeply spiritual practice.

CONCLUSION

ONE OF MY FAVORITE POEMS is by a Houston poet named Sybil Estess, the title of which is "One Thing It Was." It is illustrative of the many-and-one aspect of love and brings us logically to the conclusion of this exploration of the mystery we call love.

> *Of course it was animus projection*
> *or neurosis. It was her search for God.*
> *Her Dionysian-lack. A yen to frequent*
> *artists, a weakness for Italian males.*
>
> *Perhaps just a failure to pray?*
> *Call it recherché du temps perdu*
> *(they were fifty). It was her Dickinsonian*
> *quest for spiritual bliss, a fatal infatuation.*

It was her old trick of giving-in-order-
to-receive. Both of their failed bondings
at homes. Unfaithfulness, and guilt, and sin.
Unliberated leanings on the wrong men.

Fascination with fire and butterflies.
But then, after all labeling, fashionable
name-calling, blaming, nit-picking second
guesses, some simple, quite out-moded facts
remain: one thing it was was love.

This discussion of love in this little book is not intended to be comprehensive, but rather a contribution to the conversation about the greatest of mysteries. Mystery does not mean that something cannot be known, but it implies that the thing must be known in a non-rational or deeper level of knowing than simple ego-consciousness.

After all, it is all about energy and how that energy gets constellated, experienced, and articulated. Love is an experience of energy that can transform or destroy. That is why we must build a container called consciousness in order to direct the energy to creating rather than destroying.

Even though we only have a penlight to shed light on this cavernous concept, we must shed as much light as we can generate, for the tunnel of love can be very dark if not understood in a broader context than instinct and appetite.

Eros, Philia and Agape provide a broader viewpoint to contain this fire. The love that attracts (Eros), the love that sustains (Philia) and the love that transforms and empowers (Agape) provide the wider view.

Eros is the non-rational desire to connect, relate or create. Philia is the love of friendship that allows one to know and be known, therefore, enabling Self—knowledge through the mirror of this aspect of love. Agape is the love that lets be... not in the apathetic sense, but in the empowering sense that desires the other to be and become the truly authentic autonomous Self he/she was created to be. Agape is the love God has for us and the vehicle to experience the transcendent energy generated from the *imago Dei* deep within the soul of another.

Mother love helps determine our being. Father love empowers our competence and confidence. Other love, through Eros, Philia and Agape, helps us to evolve into the individual we were created to be. And self-love helps heal our inner divisions and is the glue to reconnect our fragmented parts.

"God is love," says St. John, and "those who dwell in love dwell in God and God in them." Jung concludes for us: "Here is the greatest and the smallest, the remotest and the nearest, the highest and the lowest, and we cannot discuss one side of it without also discussing the other. No language is adequate to this paradox. Whatever one can say, no words express the whole. To speak of partial aspects is always too much or too little, for only the whole is meaningful. 'Love bears all things and endures all things.' (I Cor. 13:7). These words say all that is to be said; nothing can be added to them."